BEVERLEY NAIDOO

Journey to Jo'burg

COLLINS
MODERN
CLASSICS

FOR AGES 9–11

Published in the UK by Scholastic, 2022
Book End, Range Road, Witney, Oxfordshire, OX29 0YD
Scholastic Ireland, 89E Lagan Road, Dublin Industrial Estate, Glasnevin, Dublin, D11 HP5F

SCHOLASTIC and associated logos are trademarks and/or registered trademarks of Scholastic Inc.

www.scholastic.co.uk

1 2 3 4 5 6 7 8 9   2 3 4 5 6 7 8 9 0 1

A CIP catalogue record for this book is available from the British Library.
ISBN 978-0702-30890-1

Printed and bound by Ashford Colour Press
Paper made from wood grown in sustainable forests and other controlled sources.

Extracts from *The National Curriculum in England, English Programme of Study* © Crown Copyright. Reproduced under the terms of the Open Government Licence (OGL). http://www.nationalarchives.gov.uk/doc/open-government-licence/version/3

Authors Sally Burt and Debbie Ridgard
Editorial team Rachel Morgan, Sarah Sodhi, Tracy Kewley and Suzanne Adams
Series designer Dipa Mistry
Typesetter QBS Learning
Cover illustrations Greg Straight/Illustration X
Illustrator Alisha Monnin/Astound
Photographs page 8: Beverley Naidoo, Keith Morris/Hay Ffotos/Alamy Stock Photo; page 18: Nelson Mandela, Wikimedia Commons; queue of people, Alamy; page 29: sign, Getty Images, passport, Alamy

Acknowledgements
The publishers gratefully acknowledge permission to reproduce the following material:
HarperCollins Children's Books for the use of the text extracts and cover from *Journey to Jo'burg* written by Beverley Naidoo
Every effort has been made to trace copyright holders for the works reproduced in this book, and the publishers apologise for any inadvertent omissions.

For supporting online resources go to:
www.scholastic.co.uk/read-and-respond/books/journey-to-joburg/online-resources
Access key: Pair

CONTENTS

How to use Read & Respond in your classroom...

Read & Respond provides teaching ideas related to a specific well-loved children's book. Each Read & Respond book is divided into the following sections:

ABOUT THE BOOK AND AUTHOR

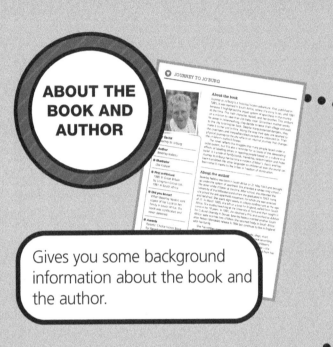

Gives you some background information about the book and the author.

GUIDED READING

Breaks the book down into sections and gives notes for using it, ideal for use with the whole class. A bookmark has been provided on page 12 containing **comprehension** questions. The children can be directed to refer to these as they read. Find comprehensive guided reading sessions on the supporting online resources.

SHARED READING

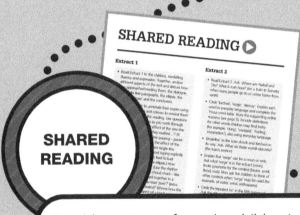

Provides extracts from the children's book with associated notes for focused work. There is also one non-fiction extract that relates to the children's book.

GRAMMAR, PUNCTUATION & SPELLING

Provides word-level work related to the children's book so you can teach grammar, punctuation, spelling and **vocabulary** in context.

PLOT, CHARACTER & SETTING

Contains activity ideas focused on the plot, characters and the setting of the story.

TALK ABOUT IT

Oracy, **fluency**, and speaking and listening activities. These activities may be based directly on the children's book or be broadly based on the themes and concepts of the story.

Provides writing activities related to the children's book. These activities may be based directly on the children's book or be broadly based on the themes and concepts of the story.

GET WRITING

ASSESSMENT

Contains short activities that will help you assess whether the children have understood concepts and curriculum objectives. They are designed to be informal activities to feed into your planning.

Online you can find a host of supporting documents including planning information, comprehensive guided reading sessions and guidance on teaching reading.

www.scholastic.co.uk/read-and-respond/books/
journey-to-joburg/online-resources
Access key: Pair

SUPPORTING ONLINE RESOURCE

Help children develop a love of reading for pleasure.

Activities

The activities follow the same format:

- **Objective:** the objective for the lesson. It will be based upon a curriculum objective, but will often be more specific to the focus being covered.

- **What you need:** a list of resources you need to teach the lesson, including photocopiable pages.

- **What to do:** the activity notes.

- **Differentiation:** this is provided where specific and useful differentiation advice can be given to support and/or extend the learning in the activity. Differentiation by providing additional adult support has not been included as this will be at a teacher's discretion based upon specific children's needs and ability, as well as the availability of support.

The activities are numbered for reference within each section and should move through the text sequentially – so you can use the lesson while you are reading the book. Once you have read the book, most of the activities can be used in any order you wish.

Section	Activity	Curriculum objectives
Guided reading		Comprehension: To participate in discussions about books that are read to them and those they can read for themselves, building on their own and others' ideas and challenging views courteously.
Shared reading	1	Comprehension: To discuss and evaluate how authors use language, considering the impact on the reader.
	2	Comprehension: To check the book makes sense to them, discussing their understanding and exploring the meaning of words in context.
	3	Comprehension: To identify and discuss themes and conventions across a wide range of writing.
	4	Comprehension: To identify how language, structure and presentation contribute to meaning.
Grammar, punctuation & spelling	1	Transcription: To spell words ending in –ant/–ance/–ancy and –ent/–ence/–ency.
	2	Vocabulary, grammar and punctuation: To use cohesive devices, such as ellipsis.
	3	Vocabulary, grammar and punctuation: To use modal verbs to indicate degrees of possibility.
	4	Comprehension: To discuss and explore the meaning of words in context.
	5	Vocabulary, grammar and punctuation: To link ideas across paragraphs using adverbials.
	6	Transcription: To spell homophones and other words that are often confused.
Plot, character & setting	1	Comprehension: To make comparisons within and across books.
	2	Comprehension: To identify and discuss themes across a wide range of writing.
	3	Comprehension: To identify and discuss conventions across a wide range of writing.
	4	Comprehension: To check the book makes sense to them, discussing their understanding and exploring the meaning of words in context.
	5	Comprehension: To read books that are structured in different ways and for different purposes.
	6	Comprehension: To draw inferences such as inferring characters' feelings, thoughts and motives from their actions and justifying inferences with evidence.
	7	Comprehension: To predict what might happen from details stated and implied.
	8	Comprehension: To ask questions to improve their understanding.

Section	Activity	Curriculum objectives
Talk about it	1	Spoken language: To participate actively in collaborative conversations, staying on topic.
	2	Spoken language: To participate in role play and improvisations.
	3	Spoken language: To use spoken language to develop understanding through exploring ideas.
	4	Spoken language: To speak audibly and fluently.
	5	Spoken language: To articulate and justify answers, arguments and opinions.
	6	Spoken language: To participate in presentations.
Get writing	1	Composition: To draft and write by selecting appropriate grammar and vocabulary, understanding how such choices can change and enhance meaning.
	2	Composition: To plan their writing by identifying the audience for and purpose of the writing, selecting the appropriate form and using other similar models for their own.
	3	Composition: To plan writing by noting and developing initial ideas, drawing on reading and research where necessary.
	4	Composition: To draft and write by using organisational and presentational devices to structure the text and to guide the reader.
	5	Composition: To draft and write by précising longer passages; to ensure consistent and correct use of tense.
	6	Composition: To evaluate and edit by assessing the effectiveness of their own and others' writing.
Assessment	1	Comprehension: To retrieve, record and present information from non-fiction.
	2	Composition: To plan their writing by identifying the audience for and purpose of the writing, selecting the appropriate form and using other similar models for their own.
	3	Spoken language: To listen and respond appropriately.
	4	Comprehension: To understand what they read by checking that the text makes sense to them, discussing their understanding and exploring the meaning of words in context.
	5	Spoken language: To use relevant strategies to build their vocabulary.
	6	Comprehension: To make comparisons within and across books.

Key facts
Journey to Jo'burg

◉ **Author**
Beverley Naidoo

◉ **Illustrator**
Lisa Kopper

◉ **First published:**
1985 in Great Britain
by Longman Group Ltd;
1991 in South Africa

◉ **Did you know?**
When Beverley Naidoo sent
copies of her book to her
family in South Africa, the
book was confiscated and
never delivered.

◉ **Awards**
Parents' Choice Honor Book
for Paperback Literature,
USA 1988
Notable Children's Trade Book
in the Field of Social Studies,
USA 1986
Child Study Children's Book
Committee Award, USA 1986
The Other Award, UK 1985

About the book

Journey to Jo'burg is a historical fiction adventure. First published in 1985, it was banned in South Africa, where the story is set, until 1991 because it highlighted the unjust system of apartheid in the country at the time. The main character, Naledi, and her brother, Tiro, embark on a mission to save their sick baby sister. Since their mother works far away in Johannesburg, they decide to leave their village and walk to the city to bring her back. Despite many potential dangers, they make it to her just in time. Along the way their eyes are opened to the cruel laws and inequalities black people are subjected to. Their physical journey to the city reflects an internal journey that changes the children's outlook forever.

The novel reflects the struggles that many people faced under a racist system, but it is also a reminder for us today of the devastating effects of labelling others or rejecting people based on a culture or a belief. It is a tale of family bonds, friendship, determination and hope. *Journey to Jo'burg* has become a modern children's classic and has been translated into other languages so children all over the world can learn what it means to live in fear or freedom of domination.

About the author

Beverley Naidoo was born in South Africa on 21 May 1943 and brought up under the system of apartheid. She attended a whites-only school – like other white children at the time. After school, she attended the University of the Witwatersrand where she graduated in 1963. Here, she joined the anti-apartheid movement, for which she was arrested and detained. She spent eight weeks in solitary confinement at the age of 21. In March 1965, she left on a boat for England, exiled from South Africa. She studied teaching at the University of York and then taught in London for 18 years. In 1991, she obtained a PhD and worked as Advisor for Cultural Diversity in Dorset. Beverley Naidoo married another South African exile and has two children. She returned freely to South Africa after Nelson Mandela's release in 1994 but continues to live in England with her family.

She has written many other novels, picture books, plays, short stories and non-fiction while also travelling and giving creative writing workshops all over the world. *Journey to Jo'burg*, her first children's book, was written in exile and she dedicated it to Mma Sebate – the woman who looked after her as a child but who was separated from her own children because of apartheid laws.

GUIDED READING ▶

Setting the scene

Introduce the book by reading the title, explaining that Jo'burg is an abbreviation of Johannesburg, the largest city in South Africa. Explore the front and back covers with the children, inviting a volunteer to read out any extract or blurb. Ask: *What genre of book do you think this is and why?* (adventure/ historical fiction: sets up an adventure/takes place in past) Use the news articles accompanying the author's note at the beginning of the book to help explain the context: apartheid was a regime in South Africa brought in by the mainly white National Party in 1948 that segregated black and other people of colour. It made laws stating what black and people of colour could and could not do. Apartheid ended in the early 1990s, culminating in the country's first democratic elections that elected its first black president, Nelson Mandela, a freedom fighter and leader of the African National Congress party (ANC) who had been imprisoned for 27 years for fighting for equal rights for all people.

Turn to the map beside the contents page in *Journey to Jo'burg* and contextualise it by showing the children a world map, indicating Africa and then South Africa. Find out what the children know already about South Africa's climate, geography, culture and way of life. Invite a volunteer to explain the map, locating the key/legend and its insert mapping the children's journey. Bearing in mind question 1 on the bookmark, read Chapter 1 together and ask a volunteer to summarise the problem and Naledi's plan. Invite subjective opinions on whether Naledi's plan was right, knowing their grandmother and aunt would not allow it. Ask: *What would you do?* As a class, build a picture of where Naledi and Tiro live and what their life is like. Ask: *How is it similar to or different from your life?* Invite initial responses to question 2 on the bookmark. The answer will become gradually clearer as the novel progresses.

On the road

Read to the end of Chapter 2, encouraging the children to empathise with Tiro and Naledi and imagine themselves undertaking a long journey to an unknown city with no money. Ask: *Do you think the children were brave or foolish?* (both) Ask: *Why did the tar road burn their feet?* (It was hot and they had no shoes.) Consider question 3 on the bookmark. Ask: *Why do you think the older children had made up a song about policemen and 'passes'?* (It reflected their lived experience: black and other people of colour were vulnerable without their passes; police could stop them any time; most people had had bad experiences relating to police and passes.) Naledi and Tiro would be fearful based on common knowledge and their uncle's experience.

Read Chapter 3, modelling fluency and expression, particularly in the dialogue, demonstrating how to 'read' the ellipsis, exclamation marks, questions and capitalised words. Ask: *Why do you think the boy helped Naledi and Tiro?* (He was also Tswana and sympathised, knowing what could happen if the white farmer caught them.) *Why do they hide the orange peel?* (They don't want the farmer to search for who stole the oranges.)

Ask the children to read Chapter 4 in groups of four, focusing on each other's use of punctuation in dialogue, as modelled in your reading of Chapter 3. Discuss question 4 on the bookmark, inviting opinions on why they trusted the boy at the orange farm and the lorry driver (he spoke the same language so was from the same tribe, Tswana; he seemed sympathetic) and whether they would accept a lift from a stranger today. Review questions 13 and 14 on the bookmark, focusing on the additional knowledge provided by the footnotes that reflects Tswana language and culture. Elicit that while the lorry driver is obviously not their father, they call him Rra as people in other communities may call an older person 'auntie', 'uncle', 'nan' or similar to show friendship and respect. 'Gogo', meaning granny, is also often used in South Africa to show an older person respect.

Johannesburg

Read to the end of Chapter 7. Johannesburg is often known as Egoli, a Sotho word meaning city of gold. Ask: *What happened to Naledi and Tiro's father? Was it a city of gold for their family?* (He died of coughing sickness – a common miners' complaint in those days; mining is still dangerous but more health and safety precautions would be in place now.) Discuss how Johannesburg is different from where the children live (endless buildings, noise, smoke, bad smells from traffic, many cars, many people). Ask: *Why did the children have to make this journey to somewhere they had never been? What would you do today instead?* (Telegram was too expensive; they had no other choice with no mobile or other phones.) Ask: *What mistake do the children make at the bus stop?* (They don't realise they can't travel on a bus designated for whites.) Explain a bit more about apartheid in South Africa at that time. Black and other people of colour didn't just need passes, there were places they couldn't go and they had separate schools with different education. Ask: *Why did Grace take the children under her wing?* (She recognises them as Tswana and wants to help. Later, it's clear she's also angry about apartheid and the lives it forces the majority of people to lead.)

Ask: *What does Mma call her employer?* (Madam) Ask: *What is Madam's reaction when she hears about Dineo?* (unsympathetic, unfair) Ask: *Why can't the children stay with their mother?* (Madam says the police would not like it; because of pass laws.) Discuss Mma's difficult decision: sending her children to Soweto, a dangerous township where black people are forced to live, with someone she barely knows.

Grace

Read the first part of Chapter 8 to 'Police!'. Remind the children of question 3 on the bookmark and invite them to predict what happens. Discuss why people were fearful (police's power and the dreaded 'passes'). Read the rest of the chapter to the children, explaining that the policeman speaks in Afrikaans, the language of many white South Africans, although also widely spoken as a second language. Model fluent and expressive reading. At the end of the chapter ask: *How did the boy*

react when he was too late with his father's pass? (He was furious, resentful, even resigned by the end.) Ask: *What does this tell you about how black people felt about their situation?* (Angry, resentful, fearful; children wondered why parents put up with it.) Explain that apartheid had been in place for more than 20 years. Older people put up with it to protect their families and earn money, but their children were beginning to feel things should be different.

Read to the end of Chapter 10 together, bearing in mind questions 5 and 7 on the bookmark. It may be difficult reading as it concerns the Soweto uprising – a series of protests led by black schoolchildren on 16 June 1976. Up to 20,000 students took part and faced police brutality; many were shot and injured or killed. Discuss question 12 on the bookmark, looking at earlier illustrations, but in particular the Chapter 10 illustration. Note that the girl near Grace who was shot was only eight years old. Come back to question 7 and link it to question 15 on the bookmark, asking: *Is Grace a real historical character?* (No, she represents many like her, looking after younger siblings while their parents worked and lived away from home; her feelings and anger would have been felt by many, especially after the uprising which was a factual event.) Invite the children to consider their school education. Everyone in England has free access to the same curriculum whatever their background – school was also not free in South Africa. It may be difficult for them to understand how passionately schoolchildren felt, not just because their learning was restricted but also because they had to learn in Afrikaans rather than their own first languages. Discuss how challenging that can be with any children for whom English is a second language in your classroom.

Returning home

Ask the children to read to the end of Chapter 11 independently, again considering question 5 on the bookmark as well as question 16. Ask: *Does Mma think differently from Grace?* (No, but she needs her job to earn money to care for her family as their father died; Grace's mother is more likely to react similarly to Mma.) Ask: *Who narrates the story?* (third person – not a character) Ask: *From whose perspective is the story told?*

(In Chapter 11 in particular, the narrator reflects Naledi's perspective – her questions, what she's seen and why her mother has never spoken about such things; it's important because the author is choosing to explain events from Naledi's perspective: as she learns about the harsh realities of life outside her village, so does the reader.

Continue reading to the end of Chapter 13. Ask: *What's the main problem for the young woman with a sick baby and for Mma with Dineo?* (They don't have enough money for good food and milk to keep their babies healthy.) Ask: *How did their hospital experience make Mma and Naledi feel?* (frightened but still hopeful) Ask: *Even if Dineo recovers, what won't change?* (the struggle to earn enough for fruit, milk and vegetables to keep Dineo healthy) Discuss with the children what is important for staying healthy (good nutrition, exercise and care). Invite the children to imagine Mma's feelings.

Read Chapter 14. Ask: *Why was Mma being home different this time?* (It was normally exciting – her visits meant fun, gifts and being with her; but now Dineo was sick.) Ask: *How did Tiro and Naledi cope with waiting?* (Tiro played with a piece of wire; Naledi tried hard not to think the worst.) Read the final chapter together, asking the children to reflect on question 17 on the bookmark. Invite them to notice Naledi's thoughts on what had happened, Grace, her school and friends. Ask: *What is Naledi's dream?* (She wants to be a doctor and save people but is aware that there may be sick children she may not be able to help.) Ask: *Why does Naledi feel she couldn't work it all out by herself?* (She is just a child beginning to understand the realities of life as a black South African girl.) Invite the children to talk about what they want to do when they leave school. Invite a discussion on question 18 on the bookmark, encouraging reasons.

Reflect on the story as a whole and together discuss questions 8 and 9 on the bookmark. The story largely follows a standard story structure, with small climaxes as well as the main climax and resolution with Dineo coming home. While discussing structure, refer to question 10 on the bookmark, looking back at the Contents. Ask: *What is the role of the chapter titles?* (They summarise each chapter's main action or feature.)

Remind the children that a theme is an idea running through a story. Discuss question 6 on the bookmark. Invite suggestions for themes, backed by evidence in the story. Link the children's suggestions to the themes of courage, hope, help, growing up and agency or power to change things. Ask: *Who showed courage in the story?* (Naledi and Tiro; Mma living apart from family; the orange farm boy and lorry driver for helping; Grace for looking after her brothers, helping the children and keeping hope alive; Dumi for fighting for freedom; the students in the uprising) Link your discussion of themes to question 11 on the bookmark and the book being historical fiction, taking place shortly after 1976. Ask: *Were any of the characters or events real?* (The characters are only based on real lives the author researched; the uprising was real.)

Less than 20 years later, South Africa elected its first black president. Things did change. Ask: *Why do you think things changed in South Africa?* (The new generation refused to accept apartheid and fought for change, like Dumi and the students and, in time, people like Naledi, who was determined to be more than a domestic worker.) Apartheid was wrong and instead of giving up, people had hope, showed courage, helped each other and eventually their collective actions led to change and new hope for a different future.

Journey to Jo'burg
by Beverley Naidoo

Focus on...
Meaning

1. What was Naledi's plan? What would you have done?

2. Why did Mma live so far away from her children for most of the year?

3. Why were Naledi and Tiro fearful of being noticed by the police? Was their fear justified?

4. Who helps Naledi and Tiro? Could they have managed without the help they got?

5. Why does Mma not talk about things in the same way as Grace?

6. What themes run through the novel?

Focus on...
Organisation

7. How does Grace's story link to the main storyline and help set the context?

8. How does the novel reflect standard story structure?

9. What is the climax of the story?

10. Why does each chapter have a title as well as a number?

SCHOLASTIC
READ & RESPOND
Helping children discover the pleasure and power of reading

Journey to Jo'burg
by Beverley Naidoo

Focus on...
Language and features

11. How does the author's note with the articles and map at the beginning of the book help you to understand the story?

12. How do the illustrations help you to appreciate the story?

13. What language reflects where and when the story is set?

14. How do the footnotes help your understanding?

Focus on...
Purpose, viewpoints and effects

15. Why is this novel called historical fiction?

16. What is the effect of the story reflecting Naledi's thoughts and understanding of events?

17. How did the journey to Johannesburg change Naledi?

18. Predict whether Naledi will fulfil her dream.

SCHOLASTIC
READ & RESPOND
Helping children discover the pleasure and power of reading

SHARED READING ▶

Extract 1

- Read Extract 1 to the children, modelling fluency and expression. Together, analyse different aspects of the text and discuss how you approached reading them: the dialogue, the single-line paragraphs, the ellipsis, the song, the 'pass' and the conclusion.

- Ask the children to annotate their copies using underlining, notes and colours to remind them how you modelled the reading. Use questions to stimulate discussion as you work through the extract: *What's the effect of the one-line paragraph starting 'On they walked…'?* (It gives the impression of time passing – pause before and after.) What is the effect of the ellipsis at the end of the next single-line paragraph? (It implies without saying explicitly that encounters with police lead to bad outcomes – pause after the ellipsis.) *How would you read the song?* (Use the rhythm in the syllables to create a choral chant – like a playground song chanted together in a rhythm.) *How would you read 'pass'?* (extra emphasis) *Why is it repeated?* (Shows how the pass governs every aspect of a black person's life). *Is the pass a good or a bad thing? How can you tell?* (It's bad for black people – most people knew someone who'd been in trouble over one; Naledi and Tiro's uncle's experience.) *How can you express this in your reading?* (serious tone, emphasise 'all too clearly')

- Discuss how the extract leads up to the concluding paragraph, moving from cheerful singing as they walk to nervous, silent hurrying.

- Now, ask the children to read the extract in pairs, using their notes to help them reflect the changes in mood. Encourage them to practise reading a piece several times to achieve their most fluent and expressive reading.

Extract 2

- Read Extract 2. Ask: *Where are Naledi and Tiro? What is rush hour?* (on a train to Soweto; when many people go to or come home from work)

- Circle 'lurched', 'surge', 'dismay'. Explain each word in everyday language and complete the 'Focus word table' from the supporting online resource (see page 5). Provide definitions for other words children may find tricky (for example, 'clung', 'wedged', 'hurling', 'commotion'), also using everyday language.

- Underline 'as the train shook and lurched on its way.' Ask: *What do these words describe?* (the train's motion)

- Explain that 'surge' can be a noun or verb. Ask what 'surge' is in the extract (noun). Invite synonyms for the context (heave, swell, flood, rush). Now ask the children to think of other contexts when 'surge' may be used (for example, of water, wind, enthusiasm).

- Circle the repeated 'no' in the fifth paragraph. Ask the effect of the repetition (emphasises children's dilemma). Explain the rule of three and how it adds emphasis to speech or description.

- Underline 'What now?' and ask the effect of ending on the unspoken (no speech marks) question (expresses children's dismay). Encourage the class to imagine the children's feelings, seeing Grace 'wedged' in the train. Invite them to add their own words to 'dismay' to express the children's feelings.

- Underline 'Police!'. Ask why the author chose a single-word paragraph (adds drama, reinforced by exclamation mark; highlights impact of police's appearance). Invite children to explain why the police's appearance would be dramatic (threat posed by pass laws).

Extract 3

- Read Extract 3 together, asking different readers to jump in at appropriate moments. Contextualise the extract in Chapter 11: the drama of their journey to Johannesburg is over. Ask: *What concern still lies ahead?* (Will Dineo recover?)

- Explain that many books involve journeys. They aren't always just physical journeys; they are often also life journeys for the protagonist – a time of growing up or transitioning. Myths and legends also sometimes involve journeys where the hero is given help, often by a supernatural being, and overcomes challenges. Ask: *What help did Naledi and Tiro get on their journey to Johannesburg?* (Poleng, orange farm boy, lorry driver, Grace)

- Invite the children to re-read the extract in groups, reflecting on Naledi's journey – her journey to Johannesburg and her personal journey and how she has grown up. Write questions on the board to guide their reading. Explain that you will discuss the questions at the end. Encourage them to underline and annotate their copies.

- Ask: *What did Naledi find confusing?* (contrasting things Mma and Grace say) *Why hadn't Mma spoken of what Grace told them?* (They were young but also she had so little time with them.) *What shows Naledi is growing up?* (her internal questions, wondering what her mother really felt, trusting she could speak to her) *What textual features bring the story to life?* (rhetorical questions, capital letters, ellipses, detail on Mma's reactions and gestures)

- At the end, discuss the questions, encouraging the children to share opinions and predictions, using words such as 'I believe that…', 'I predict…', and 'I have learned that…', backed up by evidence from the text.

Extract 4

- Hand out copies of Extract 4. Invite the children to skim the text to pick up clues and get an overall impression. Ask: *What kind of text is it? How can you tell?* (non-fiction/factual text with headings, sections and bullets) *What is the context?* (political, historical)

- Ask the children to read the text to each other, taking turns to read a sentence each to develop fluency. Ask them to use coloured pens to highlight unfamiliar words.

- Write some tricky vocabulary on the board and together find synonyms – either in the text or in a thesaurus: 'rise and fall' (success and destruction), 'apartheid' (apartness), 'restricted' (prevented), 'non-violent' (peaceful), 'exiled' (banished), 'implement' (introduce), 'uprisings' (riots/protests), 'atmosphere' (feeling in the air). Invite the children to put the words into sentences that have a different context to the one in this text. Write example sentences on the board.

- Invite the children to identify the facts in the text and highlight the key words. Remind the children that key words refer to the main verbs, nouns and adjectives.

- Discuss layout features of the text. Ask: *How do these features guide the reader?* (headings to explain each section, timeline with events in order, pictures that give a visual explanation…)

- Ask the children to identify the tense of the timeline (present tense) and compare it to the tense of the first and final paragraph (past tense). Ask: *What is the effect of using the historical present tense in the timeline?* (used to list events on a timeline and also aims to create an effect of immediacy)

Extract 1

"Come on! We must get on," Naledi insisted, pulling herself up quickly.

She could tell that Tiro was already tired, but they couldn't afford to stop for long. The sun had already passed its midday position and they didn't seem to have travelled very far.

On they walked, steadily, singing to break the silence.

But in the middle of the afternoon, when the road led into a small town, they stopped singing and began to walk a little faster. They were afraid a policeman might stop them because they were strangers.

Policemen were dangerous. Even in their village they knew that…

The older children at school had made up a song:

"Beware that policeman,
He'll want to see your 'pass'[1]*,*
He'll say it's not in order,
That day may be your last!"

Grown-ups were always talking about this "pass". If you wanted to visit some place, the "pass" must allow it. If you wanted to change your job, the "pass" must allow it. It seemed everyone in school knew somebody who had been in trouble over the "pass".

Naledi and Tiro remembered all too clearly the terrible stories their uncle had told them about a prison farm. One day he had left his "pass" at home and a policeman had stopped him. That was how he got sent to the prison farm.

So, without even speaking, Naledi and Tiro knew the fear in the other's heart as they walked through the strange town. They longed to look in some of the shop windows, but they did not dare stop. Nervously, they hurried along the main street, until they had left the last house of the town behind them.

---

1 *Every black South African over sixteen years had to carry a "passbook" at all times. It named the place where that person had to live and work.*

Extract 2

It was rush hour when they got on the train to Soweto and the children clung on tightly to Grace. There was no sitting space and it felt as if all their breath was being squeezed out of them. Grown-up bodies pressed in from above and all around them. Some people laughed, some people swore and others kept silent, as the train shook and lurched on its way.

At each station the crowd heaved towards the carriage door, people urgently pushing their way through. Naledi and Tiro tried to press backwards to stay close to Grace.

But in a sudden surge at one of the stations, they found themselves being carried forward, hurling out on to the platform. Desperately they tried to reach back to the open door, but passengers were still coming out, although the train was already beginning to move on.

Naledi was just able to see Grace wedged inside. She was trying to get out, but the train was on its way! Naledi and Tiro looked at each other in dismay. What now?

Everyone was walking towards the stairs which led to a bridge over the railway line. Soon the platform would be empty and the guard would see them. No tickets, no money, no idea of how they could find Grace. They would have to wait until she came back to get them, yet there was nowhere to hide on the platform.

"Let's go and look from the bridge," Naledi suggested.

Suddenly, without any warning, there was a commotion up ahead. Three figures in uniform stood at the top of the stairs.

Police!

Extract 3

Naledi lay with her head against her mother's shoulder. It was so confusing. Here was Mma saying that children should be in school, and there was Grace saying that schools taught black children rubbish.

Didn't Dumi and his friends carry a poster saying 'BLACKS ARE NOT DUSTBINS!'

What did Mma think about that and all the shooting? Had she heard about the little girl who was killed close to Grace? Mma had never spoken to them about such things. Did she think they were too young to be told?

Naledi stared out of the window, without seeing anything. Her mind was too full of questions. Surely she could talk to Mma about what was troubling her? As she leant against Mma's body and felt its warmth, it seemed silly to hold back problems. Especially when their time together was so short.

"Mma…" Naledi began, turning to look up at her mother's face. "Grace told us about how the schoolchildren marched in the streets…"

Naledi stopped, seeing shock and pain flash through Mma's eyes. She became even more alarmed when Mma remained quite silent for what seemed like an age, gazing down at her lap.

At last, Mma spoke very softly. "Do you know how many children died on those streets? Do you know how many mothers were crying 'Where's my child'?"

Mma was shaking her head slowly. There was another long pause, as if she was thinking whether to say any more. Then she leant forwards and covered her face with one hand, wiping her forehead.

"You know, every day I must struggle…struggle…to make everything just how the Madam wants it. The cooking, the cleaning, the washing, the ironing. From seven every morning, sometimes till ten, even eleven at night, when they have their parties. The only time I sit is when I eat! But I keep quiet and do everything, because if I lose my job I won't get another one. This Madam will say I am no good. Then there will be no food for you, no clothes for you, no school for you."

Extract 4

The rise and fall of apartheid in South Africa

Apartheid is the Afrikaans word for 'apartness'. Under apartheid, people of different cultures and colours were not allowed to be friends, get married, be in school, be on the same bus, or have fun together. People of colour had to live in certain areas, go to separate schools and do the lowest-paid jobs.

Many people in South Africa fought against apartheid for freedom. Non-violent protests turned violent and many people were arrested, exiled and lost their lives for standing up to the government. Change finally came about but it did not happen quickly or easily.

A timeline of the main events	
1948	The National Party implements the policy of apartheid
1952	Many people gather to burn their passbooks
1960	Sharpeville shooting: police open fire on peaceful protestors
1964	Rivonia trial: Nelson Mandela and other protestors sent to prison
1976	Soweto shooting: police shoot children protesting against their education
1984–89	Uprisings: South Africa declares a state of emergency
1990	Nelson Mandela is released after 27 years in prison
1994	First democratic elections are held: Nelson Mandela becomes president

Nelson Mandela at his trial (20 April 1964):

"During my lifetime I have dedicated myself to this struggle of the African people. I have fought against white domination, and I have fought against black domination. I have cherished the ideal of a democratic and free society, in which all persons live together in harmony and with equal opportunities. It is an ideal which I hope to live for and to achieve. But if needs be, it is an ideal for which I am prepared to die."

South Africa's first democratic election
On 27 April 1994, 22 million South Africans voted. There was a happy, festive atmosphere as the people of South Africa celebrated their freedom.

GRAMMAR, PUNCTUATION AND SPELLING ▶

1. Spelling patterns

Objective
To spell words ending in 'ant' and 'ent'.

What you need
Photocopiable page 22 'Spelling patterns'.

What to do

- Call out the following words, asking the children to write them in their notebooks: 'observant', 'relevant', 'decent', 'frequent', 'hesitant', 'sufficient'. Discuss the word endings, checking whether they used 'ent' or 'ant'. Find out what made them choose each ending.

- Draw two columns on the board and separate the words according to their ending. Invite children to add further words with similar sounding endings, deciding which column to put them in (for example, 'vacant', 'important', 'observant', 'brilliant', 'urgent', 'intelligent', 'innocent', 'decent').

- Explain that it can be difficult to decide which spelling to use as they sound the same but there are some clues. Invite learners to see if they can spot any guidelines ('ent' after soft 'g' or 'c' or after 'qu'; 'ant' after hard 'c' or words with a related noun ending in 'ation'). Others just have to be learned ('confident', 'independent', 'obedient').

- Ask the children to define the words' class (adjective). Organise the children into groups to complete photocopiable page 22 'Spelling patterns'. Explain that not all words have a related noun or verb, and they should leave blank any cells they cannot find an answer for. Share answers as a class and discuss how the 'e' and 'a' flow through the word family endings.

Differentiation
Support: Provide a word bank to help children complete the table.

Extension: Ask the children to choose a word family and write sentences using each word.

2. What has been left out?

Objective
To understand ellipses.

What you need
Copies of *Journey to Jo'burg*.

What to do

- Read the first page of Chapter 3. Allow everyone to read it silently first, reading for meaning to enrich children's understanding. Point out the ellipsis (…), the exclamation marks and the capital letters. Ask: *How would you incorporate these into reading aloud?* Invite volunteers to be Naledi, Tiro and the unknown boy/voice while you narrate. Practise with different volunteers.

- Explain that an ellipsis represents missing words – either using … or just omitting words that can be assumed. Ask: *What is the purpose of the ellipsis here?* (Tiro doesn't need to finish his question; Naledi knows what he'll say.) Invite a volunteer to complete his question ('Do you think we could pick an orange to eat?' or similar).

- Write 'ellipsis/ellipses' on the board pointing out the irregular plural and asking for other words following the same pattern ('oasis', 'basis', 'crisis', 'thesis'). Note that all the words have ancient Greek origins. Now organise the children into groups of four to study Chapter 13, focusing on the ellipses before reading the chapter aloud. Ask: *What is the purpose of each ellipsis?* (unspoken words or sentiments often expressing emotion and pauses, helping portray how the characters feel) *What could have been said? How did thinking about the ellipses improve your reading?*

Differentiation
Support: Allow children to work in pairs to discuss which words might replace the ellipses.

Extension: The children can repeat the exercise for Chapter 15.

3. Practise using modals

> **Objective**
> To use modal verbs to indicate possibility.
>
> **What you need**
> Copies of *Journey to Jo'burg*; photocopiable page 23 'Practise using modals'.

What to do

- Revise auxiliary/helping verbs. Ask: *Which verbs act as auxiliary verbs to form verb tenses?* ('to be' and 'to have') Invite the children to give examples of verbs in the past, future or continuous tenses. Write them on the board, discussing the verb components: auxiliary (in different tenses) plus participle (past or present), and how they indicate tense.

- Explain that modal verbs are also auxiliary verbs. They change or affect other verbs in a sentence but cannot act alone – they appear with an infinitive verb, not a participle. They do not change with number or imply tense and they have no infinitive with 'to'.

- Write the main modals on the board: 'might', 'may', 'must', 'should', 'would', 'could', 'can', 'will' and 'shall'. Invite volunteers to use them in sentences and discuss their effect. Primarily, they indicate possibility or ability, show obligation or grant permission. Discuss the difference between 'must', 'may', 'might' and 'will', and then 'should' and 'could', inviting example sentences.

- Ask the children to read Chapter 3 in groups, noting examples of modal verbs (could, can, won't, will, must, would) and the infinitive verbs they affect. Ask: *How does substituting different modals change the effect, for example 'can' for 'could' or 'should' for 'must'?* (for example, changes degree of possibility or sense of obligation)

- Talk about changing modal verbs into the negative – with and without contractions (for example 'will': 'will not'/'won't') and how to use them in questions using inversion ('Will you…?'). Then ask children to complete photocopiable page 23 'Practise using modals'.

> **Differentiation**
> **Support:** Limit the independent task to choosing and writing verbs. Then complete the rest of the sheet as a class.
>
> **Extension:** Challenge children to use modals in questions or in the negative form.

4. Working with words

> **Objective**
> To discuss and explore the meaning of words in context.
>
> **What you need**
> Focus word table from your shared reading of Extract 2.

What to do

- Mix up and display copies of the focus words ('lurched', 'surge', 'dismay') and their everyday definitions. Ask the children to match words and definitions.

- Organise children in groups. Explain that they will take turns to respond to these prompts: *Think of three things that might lurch. Describe three moments when you have felt dismay. Think of three unusual things that could have a sudden surge.* Listen to groups as they work. Choose interesting responses and ask children to share them with the class.

- Talk about children's responses, reflecting on how the activity helps to build understanding of the target words and the different contexts in which they might use the words. What emotions, if any, would they attach to the words? (For example, 'lurched' could be associated with panic – 'her stomach lurched…'.)

- Return to Extract 2 and locate the target words ('lurched', 'surge', 'dismay'). Ask: *What effect do the words create in the text?* (For example, 'lurched' implies it wasn't a smooth ride; 'surge' helps visualise the inescapable force of people exiting the train; 'dismay' expresses depth of concern.)

- Now ask the children to use the target words in their own sentences and choose their favourite to read aloud. Discuss their sentences and the mood created using the target words.

- Write the target words on the working wall. Remind the children to aim to use them in their written work.

> **Differentiation**
> **Support:** Ask the children to devise sentences in response to the prompt in pairs.
>
> **Extension:** Challenge children to find synonyms for the target words and discuss the different effect of using the synonyms in the text.

5. Time passing

> **Objective**
> To link ideas across paragraphs using adverbials.
>
> **What you need**
> Copies of *Journey to Jo'burg*.

What to do

- Discuss what everyone did at the weekend. Invite volunteers to recount their weekends. Then ask: *How did you sequence and link events? What words did you use?* (For example, 'then', 'next', 'later', 'after lunch' and so on.)

- Write the children's answers on the board, identifying adverbs and adverbial phrases or clauses – commonly classed as adverbials. Invite suggestions for other common adverbials. Ask: *What does an adverbial do?* (modifies a verb, an adjective, another adverb or a whole clause) Explain that adverbials can be of manner (how), time (when), place (where) or degree (how much), giving examples. Ask: *Which type of adverbials did you use when recounting your weekend?* (time)

- Ask the children to turn to Chapter 10 and follow you reading aloud from 'Dumi was one of those arrested' to the chapter end, modelling fluency and expression. Ask the children to focus on how the author shows time passing.

- At the end, go through, paragraph by paragraph, noting the adverbials. (For example: 'When he came out of prison'; 'Then one night'; 'For a year'; 'Until one day'; and so on.) Also point out different tenses between and within paragraphs ('had been posted'; 'was well'; 'would be coming back'; 'had written'), indicating how Grace recounts what had happened (past) and what would happen (future).

- Ask the children to write three or more paragraphs recounting their weekends, focusing on using adverbials to create a time sequence, underlining the adverbials. They can use the board and the text for examples.

> **Differentiation**
> **Support:** Provide children with a bank of common adverbials of time.
>
> **Extension:** Ask the children to summarise the story so far, linking paragraphs using adverbials of time.

6. Words in context

> **Objective**
> To distinguish between homophones in context.
>
> **What you need**
> Copies of *Journey to Jo'burg*, slips of paper, photocopiable page 24 'Words in context'.

What to do

- Begin by revising homophones. List some homophones on the board, for example: 'allowed', 'meet', 'sore', 'guessed'. Invite volunteers to suggest different ways to spell each word ('aloud', 'meat', 'saw', 'guest') and explain the differences in meanings. Ask: *What is it called when a word sounds the same but is spelled differently?* (homophone)

- Organise the children into groups, hand out slips of paper and give them five minutes to brainstorm pairs of homophones, writing each word pair on to a separate slip of paper. Bring the class together and collect the papers. Choose ten random words from the pile. Say each one aloud and ask the children to write down both spellings (or more, depending on the words chosen). Invite volunteers to use the pairs of words in sentences to demonstrate that they can differentiate between the words by using them in context.

- Re-group the children and ask them to turn to the first four paragraphs of Chapter 13. Challenge them to find as many homophones as possible (there are at least 15). Hold a plenary at the end to review the words the groups found.

- Ask the children to practise further with the homophones they found by completing photocopiable page 24 'Words in context'. Invite volunteers to read out their pairs of sentences.

> **Differentiation**
> **Support:** Give selected children a list of homophones matching the ones in the text to help them find the originals.
>
> **Extension:** Ask pairs to choose another chapter and each scan it for homophones before comparing findings.

Spelling patterns

- Complete the table of word families. Underline the word endings, looking for patterns of 'a' and 'e'.

Adjective 'ent'/'ant'	Adverb	Noun 'ence'/'ance' 'ency'/'ancy'	Verb
	tolerantly		tolerate
urgent		urgency	
		hesitation/ hesitancy	
important			
		vacancy	vacate
	expectantly		
		innocence	
	frequently		
			signify

- Naledi gains **confidence** during the story. Build a 'confidence' word family, using a dictionary to find related words. Write the word class next to each word you find.

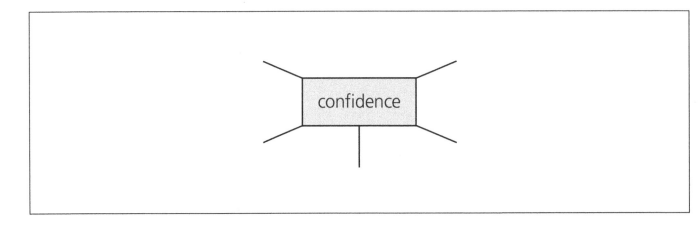

Practise using modals

- Choose a suitable modal verb to complete each sentence. Use each modal only once.

| would   couldn't   might   won't   must |

1. It _____ be ignored: they had to tell their mother.

2. Naledi decided they _____ walk to Jo'burg.

3. Naledi _____ be lying if she doesn't tell Nono.

4. The boy told them they _____ hide the orange peel.

5. If they were lucky, the police _____ not notice them.

- First, underline the modal verb and then turn the sentence into a question.

1. We could go to find Mma in Johannesburg.

_____

2. 'You can sleep here tonight,' said the boy.

_____

3. Mma should tell them things like Grace does.

_____

4. They couldn't see what was happening on the platform.

_____

- Choose five modal verbs from the box that could complete this sentence and compare the different effects:

I _____ ask Mma about what is worrying me.

| couldn't   should   may   won't   can   may not
might not   shouldn't   can't   will   could   might |

Words in context

- Write a sentence using each word from the box below in the correct context. Use a dictionary to check your work.

through	one	by	so	read	sent	too
threw	won	buy	sew	red	scent	two
						to

PLOT, CHARACTER AND SETTING ▶

1. What is it like?

> **Objective**
> To compare settings.
>
> **What you need**
> Copies of *Journey to Jo'burg*.
>
> **Cross-curricular link**
> Geography

What to do

- Pair the children to re-read Chapters 1–3. First, review the map at the front of the book. Ask: *Where do Naledi and Tiro live?* (two huts indicate the village) Ask children to draw a mind map of the area around the village, using evidence from the text (village, no running water, no doctor, track road, tar road, railway line, hills, small towns, orange trees/farm).

- Re-read Chapter 4 together, noting the scenery, matching it to the map (mountains, mine dumps). Ask: *What is the children's first impression of Johannesburg?* (endless buildings, noise, smoke, smell, many cars and people) Ask: *What are the 'tall shapes which speared up into the sky'?* (tower/office blocks) *How do the children react as the lorry slows down?* (buildings seem to be 'crowding in on them'; they feel frightened) *Why does the lorry driver give them coins?* (for the bus – too dangerous to walk)

- Discuss together the differences between the children's village and Johannesburg. Ask: *Where would you prefer to live? Why?* Encourage them to use evidence from the text and give their reasons. Now ask the children to write a paragraph comparing the two settings, ending with where they would prefer to live and why.

> **Differentiation**
> **Support:** Let children write about just one of the places.
>
> **Extension:** Ask the children to write a paragraph comparing the village or Johannesburg to where they live.

2. Identify a theme

> **Objective**
> To identify and discuss themes.
>
> **What you need**
> Copies of *Journey to Jo'burg*.

What to do

- Build on the guided reading discussion of themes. Revise the difference between a book's plot (storyline) and its theme/s (main idea/messages). Themes in children's literature tend to deal with ways to cope with common dilemmas, fears and hopes that children experience.

- Questions can help identify themes. Ask: *What does the main character learn, usually about themselves? What does the character overcome?* Write a few common themes on the board, such as friendship, overcoming adversity, growing up, family, helping others, family, hope, courage, agency and so on. Ask: *What does Naledi learn/overcome? Which themes underlie the story?* Acknowledge all answers and encourage reference to the text.

- Organise the class into groups, allocating a theme to each (courage, hope, help, growing up, agency/ power to change things). Ask them to discuss the story and find evidence for their theme – this can be done as you read the book. Model questions to guide them; for example: *Who gave the children help? What shows Naledi is growing up? Who showed courage in the story? Who inspires Naledi to think she can change how her life turns out? Why?* Explain that groups will give a short presentation on how their theme develops.

- After the presentations, ask: *Which is the most important theme?* Decide together.

> **Differentiation**
> **Support:** Ensure children are in supportive groups.
>
> **Extension:** Children can write a paragraph explaining a different theme.

PLOT, CHARACTER AND SETTING

3. Journeys in stories

Objective
To identify and discuss conventions.

What you need
Copies of *Journey to Jo'burg*.

Cross-curricular links
Geography, history

What to do

- Explain that journeys in children's literature often follow a common structure. Children must first leave home to grow and develop and only once they have gained the knowledge they need can they return. Ask the children to recall other books involving journeys and whether they follow this pattern (for example, *Charlotte's Web*, *A Single Shard*, *Percy Jackson and the Lightning Thief*, *The Firework Maker's Daughter*, *Northern Lights*).

- Discuss features of myths and legends, many of which involve journeys or quests. The hero or protagonist has to overcome a challenge and is set tests along the way before emerging a better or wiser person. Help is often provided by a supernatural being. Ask: *What features of Naledi's journey are similar to a hero's challenge?* (she has to go to Johannesburg to find their mother; faces challenges of an unknown city and of life under apartheid; receives help; grows up, during and after the journey)

- Ask: *Who helped the children?* (Poleng, farm boy, lorry driver, Grace) *Could they have managed without help?* (no) *What tests are they set?* (lack of money, distance, avoiding police, finding shelter and food, finding their way in Johannesburg, apartheid rules)

- Organise the children into groups to discuss: *What knowledge did Naledi gain and how was she changed at the end of her journey?* Allow time to discuss ideas before sharing as a class. Now ask them to write two paragraphs: one summarising the actual journey; the other explaining how Naledi's personal journey changed her.

Differentiation
Support: Ask pairs to write a paragraph each.

Extension: Invite children to also write a paragraph about Tiro and if he changed.

4. Historical context

Objective
To explore a historical setting.

What you need
Copies of *Journey to Jo'burg*, photocopiable page 29 'Historical context', Extract 4, paper.

Cross-curricular link
History

What to do

- Revise what the children have learned about apartheid from the story and Extract 4. Ask: *When did apartheid end?* (1994; first democratic elections) *When was the book set? How can you tell?* (soon after 1976 Soweto uprising – Grace's story) *What do we call stories set in the past based on real-life events?* (historical fiction)

- Ask the children to read photocopiable page 29 'Historical context' in groups. Explain that pass laws, education and the police are three important aspects of apartheid featured in the book and that they are doing historical research to understand the story context better. Encourage them to think of questions to ask after their reading. After reading, invite groups to share and discuss their questions.

- If it isn't mentioned, point out that the terms used to categorise people are not necessarily ones we would use today in the UK. Explain that each country uses words differently and, in this case, they have special meaning in South African history.

- Now ask groups to divide their paper into three columns headed 'Passes', 'Police' and 'Education'. They should then make notes of instances when each features in the story and how they affect Naledi's and Tiro's lives. Ask: *How is reading this book a good way to learn about history?* Invite children to give their opinions using evidence from the story.

Differentiation
Support: Groups can focus on one or two of the aspects of apartheid.

Extension: Children can prepare a presentation on the benefit of using historical fiction to understand history, with *Journey to Jo'burg* as an example.

5. Introducing Chapter 1: Naledi's plan

Objective
To explore plot structure.

What you need
Copies of *Journey to Jo'burg*.

Cross-curricular links
History, PSHE

What to do

- Ask: *How do you find out about a book before reading it?* (cover illustrations, blurb, extract, reviews) Ask: *What's the role of an introduction?* (introduces characters, sets the scene) Explain that this book has additional information to help set the scene.

- Ask the children to read the introductory text in italics before the story, and the news articles. Ask: *Who's speaking in the text?* (author) *What inspired this story?* (articles about children trying to be with family) *Why did she write it?* (to help children understand life for many black children under apartheid)

- Turn to the map and invite volunteers to explain how the map also helps set the context (shows how far away Mma and the hospital are, emphasises the enormity of the children's decision).

- If the edition contains a biographical note about Beverley Naidoo or a foreword by Michael Rosen, read them as a class or explain that the author was exiled from South Africa for disagreeing with apartheid. The book, written in the early 1980s, was banned in South Africa until 1991 when apartheid was already ending. Ask: *Why do you think the government banned the book?* (may encourage black people to fight against apartheid)

- Re-read Chapter 1 with you narrating and volunteers as Naledi and Tiro. Ask: *What problem do the children face?* (sister sick, far from hospital, no money for doctor, Mma in Johannesburg). Ask the children to write a short newspaper article, similar to those in the book, about the children's journey to find their mother.

Differentiation
Support: Provide children with a frame for the article, using sentence starters.

Extension: Ask children to explain why the author included the introductory information.

6. Mma and Grace

Objective
To compare and contrast characters.

What you need
Copies of *Journey to Jo'burg*, photocopiable page 30 'Mma and Grace'.

What to do

- Re-read Chapter 6 to '…the children began their story'. Ask: *Why does the young woman (Grace) tell the children they shouldn't be sorry?* (It's unfair they can't use all the buses.) *Who does she mean by 'those stupid people'?* (the white people on the bus and the white government responsible for apartheid) *Why do the children think she's different to Mma?* (Mma never spoke out angrily.)

- Organise the children into pairs. Hand out photocopiable page 30 'Mma and Grace'. Explain that they are going to skim through Chapters 6–11, making notes about Mma and Grace – one character each – noting what they are like, age, how they speak, what they do, how they feel, their families, what their situations are.

- Remind them that they are reading the story through the children's eyes. Ask: *How do Naledi's views about her mother change and why?* (She begins to realise Mma may feel like Grace but she has to keep silent to keep her job to look after her family.)

- After finishing their notes, they should discuss the characters, noting similarities and differences before completing their worksheets with a paragraph comparing the two characters. Invite volunteers to share their paragraphs with the class.

Differentiation
Support: Discuss the similarities and differences with children before they write their paragraph.

Extension: Children can write another paragraph explaining why Grace seems angrier and speaks out more than Mma.

7. What did she say?

What to do

- Re-read Chapter 15 in chunks to the children, modelling fluency, expression and mood. After each chunk, discuss any reading strategies used and ask children to copy read in pairs, giving each other feedback about fluency. At the end, discuss the overall mood and link it to the chapter title 'Hope'. Ask: *Was the chapter hopeful all the way through?* (No, the worry about Dineo and how to pay back money, among other worries, dominates.) *What creates the feeling of hope?* (Naledi's thoughts and questions help her to visualise a different, better future, and finding others like Grace.)

- Focus on the ellipsis in the penultimate paragraph and ask: *What had Naledi found out?* (Acknowledge all answers and guide the children to see Naledi at the beginning of a new journey, fighting for a better education and a fairer world where she could be whatever she wanted to be without apartheid.)

- Re-read the last sentence of the chapter and encourage the children to visualise being Naledi back at school, surrounded by friends 'old and new'. Imagine initial greetings, and then ask: *What would Naledi say about her journey? How would she find new friends like Grace?* Have a class discussion, inviting suggestions for things Naledi would include when recounting her journey and the changes in her understanding. Finally, ask the children to write what Naledi said to her friends, starting with: 'You'll never guess what happened to me! It all started when…'

8. Questions

What to do

- Ask: *Why do we ask questions?* (to find something out) Ask: *From whose perspective is this story told?* (the children's, mainly Naledi's) Explain that the author uses questions that Naledi asks herself to demonstrate her growing understanding of the world she lives in. Read the last page of Chapter 4, highlighting what Naledi asked Mma and later herself. Ask: *What does this tell you about Naledi?* (She doesn't fully understand apartheid, living in their village, but is beginning to question why things are the way they are – a sign of growing up.) Now read Chapter 11 from 'Vast stretches of land…' to the end. Ask: *What does this passage tell you about Naledi?* (She understands more and realises how little she knows about her mother and her struggles.)

- Ask groups to scan Chapters 7, 10, 11, 12, 13 and 15 to find other questions Naledi asks herself. Having found her questions, invite children to discuss what events or people prompted Naledi to question things, then share their ideas as a class.

- Now ask: *Thinking about the story, what would you have asked if you were Naledi? For example, after hearing Grace's story: Is it fair that black and white children get taught differently?* Encourage the children to pinpoint when in the story they would have asked their questions.

- Hand out photocopiable page 31 'Questions'. Explain they will answer some of Naledi's questions, using what they have learned from the story and about apartheid in South Africa.

Historical context

After winning the election in 1948, using the slogan 'apartheid', the Afrikaner National Party began controlling the majority black people and other people of colour by limiting where they could go and what they could do.

The minority white government passed laws requiring everyone to be classified as 'White', 'Bantu' (black), 'Coloured' (mixed race) or 'Other/Indian'. The government then passed more laws to maintain control and power:

- People from different races weren't allowed to marry or be in a relationship.

- People of colour were moved from their homes if they lived in a designated white area (mostly urban) and forced to live in townships, such as Soweto, Langa or Gugulethu.

- The Bantu education system limited what black and other children of colour were allowed to learn in school. The 1976 Soweto uprising of black schoolchildren protested at being forced to learn in Afrikaans rather than in their own languages.

- The Pass Laws Act of 1952 forced all black and other South Africans of colour aged over 16 to carry a passbook everywhere and at all times.

The police enforced these unfair laws and suppressed all opposition. They often used violence and force, creating an atmosphere of fear. The pass or dompas (dumb pass) was like a passport. It contained a person's fingerprints, photograph, employment details, permission to be in a particular area, permission to work or look for work in the area and employer reports on how well a person was working.

If you forgot your pass or it was lost or stolen, you could be arrested and imprisoned. Often families were separated because they did not have 'permission' in their passes to be in the same areas. More than 250,000 black people were arrested every year under the Pass Laws which made the pass one of the most hated symbols of apartheid and black oppression.

Mma and Grace

- Make notes on Mma and Grace using Chapters 6–11.

Notes on Mma	Notes on Grace
What they are like, their age, how they speak, what they do, how they feel, their families, what their situations are and so on.	

- Write a paragraph comparing the two characters.

Mma is similar to Grace…

_____
_____
_____
_____
_____
_____

However, she is also different because…

_____
_____
_____
_____
_____
_____

Questions

- Answer Naledi's questions using your knowledge from the story and what you learned about apartheid in South Africa.

1. Why can't we live with you in the city? We could go to school there, couldn't we?... But why not? Why not? (Chapter 4)

_____

_____

_____

2. Why does the white lady seem cross with Mma? (Chapter 7)

_____

_____

_____

3. Why couldn't Mma have left straight away, and what if something happened to Dineo before they arrived? (Chapter 10)

_____

_____

_____

4. What if they got there just a minute too late. That couldn't happen...could it? (Chapter 12)

_____

_____

_____

5. Wasn't it possible that in her own school there were people like Grace? (Chapter 15)

_____

_____

_____

6. Where would she, the doctor, get food for the baby?...What could she do? (Chapter 15)

_____

_____

- Add your own question that you would ask on the back of the sheet and then answer it.

TALK ABOUT IT ▶

1. Journey checklist

Objective
To participate actively in collaborative conversations, staying on the topic.

What you need
Copies of *Journey to Jo'burg*, photocopiable page 35 'Journey checklist'.

Cross-curricular links
PSHE, geography

What to do
- Read Chapter 1 from 'Finally Naledi could stand it no longer' to the chapter end, modelling fluency and expression. Ask: *What is Naledi's plan?* (to walk to Johannesburg) *What did or didn't the children know before setting off?* (vague idea of distance, hoping to get food on way) *What did Poleng ask about their journey?* ("How will you eat on the way?") *What questions could they have asked themselves about the trip before setting off?* (Where will we sleep? How long will it take?)

- Invite the children to think about a journey they've embarked on. Ask: *Who did the planning? What transport did you use? How long did it take? What did you take with you?*

- Organise the children into small groups. Hand out photocopiable page 35 'Journey checklist'. Groups can choose a destination from the examples provided or one of their own.

- Ask the groups to discuss what they might need for their journey and make a list of ten items in order of importance. Suggest group roles to encourage active participation and focus on the topic.

- Invite groups to present their checklist to the class, giving reasons/explanations for their choices.

Differentiation
Support: Let children plan and describe their own daily journey to school.

Extension: Pairs plan a school trip to a city near them and present it to the class.

2. Pleased to meet you

Objective
To participate in role play and improvisations.

What you need
Copies of *Journey to Jo'burg*.

Cross-curricular link
PSHE

What to do
- Ask the children to skim Chapter 1 and identify the conversations – the characters and topic of discussion, for example Naledi and Nono discuss Dineo; Naledi explains her idea to Tiro; Naledi and Tiro tell Poleng about their plan.

- Discuss how conversation topics and tone vary according to who is speaking to whom (child to child, child to familiar adult or child to stranger). Ask: *How do you speak to elders, friends or strangers?* (Discuss, for example, different ways of greeting.) If appropriate, compare communication on social media platforms. Ask: *How is this type of communication different from real life? Invite responses.*

- Ask: *What's the difference between reading a dialogue in a story and acting it out?* (when acting, we may need to improvise and fill in parts of dialogue that the author may have omitted)

- List on the board three or four important things to remember when acting in front of an audience (speak clearly, face audience, use expression, learn words, speak in character).

- Children work in pairs or small groups to role play a conversation from the story. Remind them to use their own words and improvise where necessary.

- Children present their role play to the class.

Differentiation
Support: Children act out the dialogue in the book with a narrator reading the narrative text.

Extension: Role play an imaginary conversation that might have taken place in the story.

3. Who's in charge?

Objective
To use spoken language to develop understanding through exploring ideas.

What you need
Photocopiable page 36 'Who's in charge', copies of *Journey to Jo'burg*.

Cross-curricular link
PSHE

What to do

- Read Chapter 7 together, inviting different children to jump in and read as you go. Ask volunteers to explain the term 'Madam' and give a synonym (a formal term used for women of rank; boss, owner, employer).

- Compare the Madam to Mma through the eyes of the children. Ask: *What did the children notice about Madam?* (unsympathetic, bossy, dismissive, cross) *What seemed strange about the way she spoke to Mma?* (appeared cross with Mma about Dineo being sick) *Did the children feel welcome in Madam's house? Explain.* (No, Mma wore a strange uniform and had separate plates and mugs; they were not allowed to stay there.)

- In pairs, ask the children to skim the book and list the adults that Naledi and Tiro meet or hear about on their journey (farmer, lorry driver, Grace, Madam, policeman, Dumi, young woman and baby, doctor). The story is told through the children's eyes. Discuss how the children view these adults. Ask: *What role do the adults have in the story? Which adults did the children like or admire? Which adults helped them? Which adults scared them?*

- Hand out photocopiable page 36 'Who's in charge?'. Invite the children to explore the various characters and express their ideas and opinions based on the text.

- Have a class feedback. Each group chooses an adult character to describe to the class in detail.

Differentiation
Extension: Compare two adults that represented the divisions in society at the time, like Madam and Mma. Compare their lives and what they could or could not do according to the law.

4. Eyewitness account

Objective
To speak audibly and fluently.

What you need
Copies of *Journey to Jo'burg*.

Cross-curricular link
PSHE

What to do

- Read Chapter 8 from 'Everyone was walking towards the stairs' to 'Let's hurry then!'. Read to the class, demonstrating expression and fluency. Discuss the techniques used (in text and reading) to create the tensions and emotions, for example, short sentences, words such as 'urgently', 'whispered', 'screamed' and the use of exclamations.

- Ask the children to take turns to re-read the text to a partner using the strategies modelled. Listeners should comment on how well their partner read and highlight any issues. Then invite the class to re-read the text chorally, demonstrating expression and fluency.

- Focus on comprehension. Ask: *What is happening? Where are they? Who's in trouble? Why? Do you think the police were doing their job? What words describe how the boy felt as he was handcuffed? What word class is 'commotion'? What does it mean?* Use 'commotion' in another context, for example, school. Find verbs in the text describing how people moved to get away from the police ('running', 'leapt', 'scrambled', 'sprinted', 'clambered').

- Ask pairs to retell the event as an eyewitness (someone who was watching the scene). They can use phrases such as 'I saw…', 'It looked like…', 'The people were…', 'I noticed…', 'I could see…'.

- Ask the pairs to give each other feedback on how interesting, audible and fluent their partners were.

Differentiation
Support: Let children tell a familiar event from their lives, using expression and speaking audibly and fluently.

Extension: Ask the children to retell the scene from a different character's viewpoint using first-person pronouns (for example, Naledi, Tiro, the young boy who was handcuffed or the old woman pushed into the van).

5. Freedom!

Objective
To articulate and justify answers, arguments and opinions.

What you need
Photocopiable page 37 'Freedom!', dictionaries and thesauruses, copies of *Journey to Jo'burg*.

Cross-curricular link
History

What to do

- Read Chapter 10 together. Ask the children to identify the theme in the chapter/story (freedom).

- Trigger their thoughts by asking: *What does freedom mean?* Invite personal responses, making notes on the board with key words and phrases, for example, no rules, opposite of captivity, no work, doing whatever suits you and so on. Ask them to list what freedom is and what it is not.

- Write the following characters' names on the board: Dumi, Grace, Mma, Madam. Ask small groups to discuss: *What does freedom mean to each character? Do you think they are free? Why?* Have a short report back.

- Invite children's views and opinions using sentence stems such as: 'Freedom means…', 'I feel free when…', 'I am/am not free (at school or home) because…', 'I think some people limit my freedom because…'.

- Hand out photocopiable page 37 'Freedom!'. Explain how to create an acrostic for the word 'freedom'. For each letter they must write a single word or phrase to describe freedom in their own way. They can use dictionaries and thesauruses to find words/ideas.

- Groups take turns to share their acrostic with the class (for example, F = fearlessness in the face of authority; R = respecting each other's right to be free; E = each and every person; E = enjoy it; D = don't be afraid to speak out; O = opinions count, be free of others' opinions; M = make it happen).

Differentiation
Support: Make two lists of synonyms and phrases to describe freedom and captivity.

Extension: In pairs, use the non-fiction extract to make an acrostic with the word 'apartheid'.

6. Hope for the future

Objective
To participate in presentations.

What you need
Copies of *Journey to Jo'burg*.

Cross-curricular link
PSHE

What to do

- Read Chapter 15. Ask: *Why do you think the chapter is called 'Hope'? Who feels hopeful? Why?*

- Together, discuss the following questions: *Why did Mma have to return to Johannesburg? What was her job? Does Mma like her job? Why doesn't she leave and find another, better job? What job does Tiro think he could do? What stops him? What sentence describes how the children in Soweto feel about their future? What does Naledi decide she wants to be one day? Why does she want to do this job? What challenges does she identify?*

- Ask volunteers to name some jobs (occupations or services) that interest and inspire them. Make a list. Discuss the pros and cons of various jobs and the challenges involved. Ask: *Do you know someone who does their job really well? Is there someone who helps or inspires you?*

- Working individually, ask the children to research one or more jobs they find interesting. They could interview someone to find out more about what the job entails. They should then prepare a speech about a job – what it involves, what qualifications or training you need, the pros and cons, an example of someone they know who does this job. Their speech should have an introduction and a conclusion.

- After each speech, children can answer questions from the class about their job.

Differentiation
Support: Provide sentence stems such as: *This job involves…, For this job you need…, The pros and cons are…*

Extension: Challenge the children to create a multimedia advertisement for a job. Include a job description and the skills and characteristics needed for the job. List the pros and benefits to be enjoyed.

Journey checklist

• In groups, choose a destination that appeals to you and
then plan your journey by answering the questions below.

> an island holiday   an African safari   an Arctic expedition

1. Where are you going?

_____

_____

2. How will you get there?

_____

_____

3. How long will the trip take? Will you need a stopover?

_____

_____

4. What will you eat on your trip?

_____

_____

5. What will the weather be like?

_____

_____

6. Where will you stay? Who will you stay with?

_____

_____

• List ten items you will pack in order of importance.

Most important	
1	6
2	7
2	8
4	9
5	10
	Least important

Who's in charge

- Discuss and make notes on the adults in the story.

- Ask yourself: *Who or what were they in charge of? How did they behave towards others? Who did the children like and who were they afraid of?*

- Write a conclusion. Explain what the children learned from the adults about their situation in South Africa.

The lorry driver (Chapter 4)	The farmer (Chapter 3)
Grace (Chapters 6–10)	Madam (Chapter 7)
Dumi (Chapters 9–10)	Mma (Chapters 7–15)
The doctor (Chapter 13)	The policeman (Chapter 8)

Freedom!

- In pairs, discuss what freedom means to you.
- Use dictionaries and thesauruses to find definitions and synonyms.
- Use your ideas to create an acrostic on freedom.
- Prepare to read it aloud to the class with expression.

F	
R	
E	
E	
D	
O	
M	

GET WRITING ▶

1. An urgent message

> **Objective**
> To draft and write for a specific purpose.
>
> **What you need**
> Copies of *Journey to Jo'burg*, photocopiable page 41 'An urgent message'.
>
> **Cross-curricular link**
> History

What to do

- Read Chapter 1 together using either choral reading or the jump-in reading technique.

- Ask: *Who knows what a telegram is?* (an electronic message sent by telegraph, printed and delivered) Explain that the sender was charged per character, so messages were usually short and without punctuation and had to be clear. Talk about how communication has changed (replaced by emails and text messages).

- Discuss the challenges of communication before mobile phones. Ask: *Why didn't Naledi phone Mma? Why did Nono not want to send a telegram? Why couldn't the children send a telegram? How is texting similar and different?* (Both have abbreviated words and missing punctuation but texting includes emojis, informal jargon and more words.) Discuss ideas for what Naledi and Tiro's telegram might have said (for example, *Dineo v sick pls come home*).

- Explain that they must summarise the main idea and write a modern text message from Naledi to Mma using a limited number of words (for example 50–60 words) and language to suit the purpose.

- Hand out photocopiable page 41 'An urgent message'. Invite children to draft their messages then read them aloud. Encourage feedback (is the message effective, too long/too short?).

> **Differentiation**
> **Support:** Let pairs edit the message.
>
> **Extension:** Challenge the children to write Mma's reply.

2. To whom it may concern

> **Objective**
> To plan writing by selecting the appropriate form.
>
> **What you need**
> Copies of *Journey to Jo'burg*.
>
> **Cross-curricular link**
> PSHE

What to do

- Read together Chapters 12–13. Invite the children to describe the conditions at the hospital. Skim the text for clues. Ask: *Why do you think the conditions were so bad?*

- Tell the children that they are going to draft a formal letter to the manager of the hospital to complain about the unacceptable conditions the patients experience there.

- Revise key features of letter writing, including layout. Remind them that this is a formal letter, so the language and grammar need to be appropriate.

- To plan the content, children should note down three key issues they want to highlight, for example long queues and waiting, too few staff, lack of assistance, nowhere to sit, no food or clean water and so on.

- Using these ideas, invite the children to draft a letter to be sent to the person in charge. They can make up a name or use the starting line 'To whom it may concern'.

- When they have finished, invite the children to read aloud their letters to their partner, checking each other's work to see if it contains the necessary information and if the tone and language are appropriate.

> **Differentiation**
> **Support:** Ask the children to work in pairs.
>
> **Extension:** Challenge the children to write a reply from the hospital manager.

3. Beware!

Objective
To note and develop initial ideas.

What you need
Photocopiable page 42 'Beware!', copies of *Journey to Jo'burg*.

Cross-curricular link
Drama

What to do
- Read Chapter 2 from 'But in the middle of the afternoon' to the end. Discuss the context. Ask: *What were Naledi and Tiro afraid of?* (policeman) *What happened to their uncle?* (he was sent to a farm prison) *Who made up the song?* (older children at school) *Why?* (as a warning – to make everyone aware)

- Relate this to children's own lives. Ask: *Do you know any other safety songs or rhymes with a warning?* Discuss familiar examples, such as 'Stop says the red light, go says the green, be careful says the yellow light blinking in between'.

- Talk about the rhythm. Clap the beat and show how it can be chanted. Identify the rhyming words ('pass', 'last') and the rhyming pattern (a,b,c,b).

- Identify other dangers the children faced, for example, the farmer on the orange farm (Chapter 3), the ride in the back of the lorry (Chapter 4), getting lost in the crowded train (Chapter 8).

- Hand out photocopiable page 42 'Beware!'. Explain they should plan a 'Beware' verse about one of the 'dangers' discussed. Encourage creative ideas. Allow time for drafting and editing.

- Invite volunteers to read or perform their verses to the class and invite constructive feedback.

Differentiation
Support: Model the writing of a verse, for example: *Beware of the farmer – he's a very angry man. If you hear him coming, you really better scram!*

Extension: Create one song with four or five verses covering the different dangers.

4. A healthy meal plan

Objective
To use organisational and presentational devices to structure the text and guide the reader.

What you need
Photocopiable page 43 'A healthy meal plan', copies of *Journey to Jo'burg*.

Cross-curricular links
PSHE, science

What to do
- Read Chapter 13 from 'Did he say Dineo will get better, Mma?' to the end. Ask: *What advice did the doctor give Mma?* (to give Dineo milk, fruit and vegetables) *Why was this a challenge for her?* (not enough money) *Will she follow this advice? Why?* (only if she can save enough money)

- Relate the doctor's advice to children's own lives. Find out what food they enjoy and what they like to eat for breakfast and dinner. Ask: *What types of food do you like? Do you help to do the shopping? Do you eat something healthy each day? Do you enjoy healthy or unhealthy food?*

- In pairs, invite the children to make two lists: healthy and non-healthy foods they usually eat. Include drinks and snacks. Share ideas with the class.

- Explain that they will create a healthy meal plan for their own family for four days. The meal plan should include a variety of fruit and vegetables and healthy meal ideas.

- Hand out photocopiable page 43 'A healthy meal plan'. Discuss ways to organise the meal plan with headings for each day, sections and bullets. They can include pictures or a diagram showing a healthy lunch box with labels for each item. Display the meal plans for everyone to enjoy.

Differentiation
Support: Ask the children to focus on creating one meal for themselves, for example, school lunch.

Extension: Children could create a cost-effective meal plan for Naledi's family for the week. Provide a budget and get them to include the cost of the items on the menu.

5. Timelines

Objectives
To draft and write by précising longer passages and to ensure use of the correct tense.

What you need
Extract 4, copies of *Journey to Jo'burg*.

Cross-curricular link
History

What to do

- Read Extract 4 to the children, modelling fluency. Focus on the timeline. Ask: *How is the timeline organised?* (chronological order) *What is the purpose of this timeline?* (to summarise important dates) *Is it complete?/Does it have all the details of that period? Why?* (No, you cannot fit all the dates and details on to a timeline – only key events that support your topic/text.) *Which direction/layout does the timeline follow?* (vertical but could be horizontal)

- Ask the children to identify the tense in the timeline (present tense). Explain that the information on a timeline can be written in the past or present tense, but the main thing is that it should be consistent. In pairs, invite the children to change the timeline (in Extract 4) from the present tense to the past tense. Share with the class.

- Working individually, ask the children to create a timeline of main events in the story. They should skim the book and identify six to eight key events from the story. They can choose the format and the tense for their timeline presentation. Provide time for drafting and editing.

- Afterwards, invite the children to swap with a partner and check each other's work.

Differentiation
Support: Provide children with three or four key events on a timeline and ask them to add three or four events of their own.

Extension: Ask children to include an event from each chapter in the timeline. Alternatively, they could create a timeline of their own life including significant events.

6. An interactive review

Objective
To assess the effectiveness of their own and others' presentation of a book review.

What you need
Poster paper, copies of *Journey to Jo'burg*.

What to do

- Tell the children that they are going to design and present an interactive book review poster to display in class, giving information and opinions about the book.

- On the board, note different aspects to consider in a book review: characters, plot, setting, genre, interesting vocabulary, themes, audience and personal opinions or rating. In groups, children discuss and make notes.

- Come back to discuss ideas to present information interactively, for example, creating a city scene with rooftops that flip up to reveal text, concertina strips that extend, pegs or pins to fasten notes, paper bins or envelopes with hidden information, wheels that turn to reveal text and windows that open.

- Working individually, ask the children to plan a review poster with facts and their opinions about the book. They can then create their final draft on poster paper.

- Display the reviews. Invite everyone to read each one and decide on the most effective review based on criteria such as: Is the title of the book obvious? Is the plot clear? Does the review cover all aspects of the book? Is it comprehensive? Is there good detail? Is the opinion backed by good reasons? Is it fun to read? Are there great interactive ideas to keep the reader engaged? Rate them with five stars for each aspect.

Differentiation
Support: Provide children with a book review template.

Extension: Challenge the children to promote the book using positive, persuasive language.

An urgent message

- List key issues that must be communicated from Naledi to Mma.

- Write a short, modern text message using 60 words or fewer to communicate your message clearly, without ambiguity.

Key issues

Text message

Beware!

- Use this sheet to plan a verse about a dangerous person or place that the children had to be wary of in the story.

The topic of the verse is:

_____

_____

The purpose is:

_____

_____

Who will sing it?

_____

_____

Interesting words that describe this person or place:

_____

_____

Interesting comparisons I could use (similes and metaphors):

_____

_____

Some rhyming words:

_____

_____

The rhyming pattern will be:

_____

_____

My first draft:

_____

_____

_____

_____

A healthy meal plan

Create a healthy meal plan for a family for four days. Organise it including headings for each meal, bullets and any other necessary information, for example, a shopping list, optional extras.

Day 1	Day 2

Day 3	Day 4

Extra information

ASSESSMENT ▶

1. This is me

Objective
To retrieve, record and present personal information as a formal, non-fiction source.

What you need
A passport, copies of *Journey to Jo'burg*.

Cross-curricular links
Geography, PSHE

What to do

- Ask the children to skim the text to recap the parts of the story mentioning the 'pass'. Ask: *What was the 'pass'?* (an identity document) *Who had to have it and why?* (people of colour who wanted to work or travel in 'whites only' areas)

- Discuss why citizens have a passport. Ask: *What is the purpose of a passport? How is it similar and different to the pass in the story?* (both control movement between places; only people of colour were required to have a pass)

- In pairs, ask the children to discuss what information appears in a passport. List questions such as: *What is your full name? Where were you born? Where do you live now? What is your occupation/status? What do you look like?* Share ideas as a class.

- Tell the children that they are going to create an imaginary school passport that they can use to visit another school. They should include factual information about who they are, where they live, the name of their current and previous schools, their age, clubs they belong to, sports they play, books they've read and so on.

- Assess the children's ability to retrieve, record and present the information effectively.

Differentiation
Support: Provide a template.

Extension: Children design a 'Passport to Read' with the names of books they've read and places mentioned in the stories.

2. Naledi's diary

Objective
To identify the audience for and purpose of the writing.

What you need
Copies of *Journey to Jo'burg*.

What to do

- Invite a discussion about diary writing. Ask: *Who keeps a diary? What type of diary is it? What is the purpose of a diary?* (to record daily events and express personal feelings and opinions) *What features of diary writing can you remember?* (personal style, informal language, first-person narrative, details of thoughts/feelings, illustrations)

- Compare and discuss the style used to tell the story. Ask: *What style does the author use?* (narrative – story is told by third-person narrator) *Could the story have been told in diary form? How would it change?* Invite opinions.

- Invite the children to choose a chapter to write a diary entry from Naledi's perspective. They should begin by skimming and scanning the chapter and noting what happens and in what order. Their notes can include details from the chapter but also other ideas they might want to include, for example Naledi's thoughts and feelings. Encourage creativity.

- Working individually, ask the children to use their notes to write a diary entry in the first person.

- Afterwards, they should share their work with a partner and give constructive feedback about the style and content of the diaries.

Differentiation
Support: Provide sentence starters such as: 'I saw…', 'I thought…', 'I felt…', 'I couldn't believe it when…'.

Extension: Let children choose another character to write a diary entry for.

3. A new friend

Objective
To listen and respond appropriately.

What you need
Copy of *Journey to Jo'burg*.

What to do

- Explain to the children that they will listen to a text and then demonstrate their understanding of the text by completing an activity based on what they hear.

- Set the scene by asking: *What did the children plan to do when they got to Jo'burg? Did they have any idea what to expect? How did the bus driver help them?* Invite responses.

- Before reading the text, write some question words on the board (Who? What? Where? When? Why?) as a reminder of the kinds of things to notice.

- Read aloud Chapter 6, modelling fluency and expression. Afterwards, check the children's understanding of various words in context by asking them to come up with synonyms for these words: 'startled', 'pavement', 'trundled'. What did Grace mean by 'You must be strangers here' and what did Mma mean by 'She thinks I belong to her mother'? Invite responses.

- Read the chapter again. Remind the children to listen for details (and make notes if necessary).

- Invite the children to do one of the following activities in response to the text: list the events in order with as much detail as possible or summarise the extract in a paragraph using their own words.

- Assess their ability to listen, retrieve information and demonstrate their understanding.

Differentiation

Support: As they listen, encourage the children to create a mind map with key words to remember the details.

Extension: Ask the children to write questions about the chapter then swap questions and answer them.

4. Grace's story

Objective
To discuss their understanding and explore the meaning of words in context.

What you need
Copies of *Journey to Jo'burg*, photocopiable page 47 'Grace's story'.

What to do

- Open by telling the children that they are going to do a comprehension activity. Begin by asking: *How did the children meet Grace? Why did Mma let Grace take the children for the night? Did she have any other option? Did Mma know they would be safe?* Invite their responses.

- Prepare the children to answer the comprehension questions. Discuss and then list comprehension technique on the board: read the text and questions carefully, identify lower to higher order questions (questions that require explicit answers that can be found in the text to questions that require inference and opinions based on the text), skim for clues, scan for detail, check the meaning of unfamiliar words in context, re-read the questions and text before answering in full sentences.

- Together, read Chapter 10, modelling expression and fluency. Re-read the text together as a choral reading to develop their fluency and understanding. Hand out photocopiable page 47 'Grace's story'. Read the instructions and questions aloud. Ensure the children are comfortable with the context and general meaning without giving specific answers.

- Invite the children to complete the comprehension, using *Journey to Jo'burg* Chapter 10 for reference.

- Check their answers to assess their comprehension skills and ability to work independently.

Differentiation

Support: Let the children choose specific questions from those provided and allow them to answer without using full sentences so they focus on the answer rather than the grammar, spelling and punctuation.

Extension: Invite the children to summarise the extract in their own words with word limits as appropriate.

5. Vocabulary counts

Objective

To use relevant strategies to build their vocabulary.

What you need

Copies of *Journey to Jo'burg*, Word list – Years 5 and 6 (English Appendix 1 – Spelling, National Curriculum), dictionaries, thesauruses.

What to do

- Begin by asking the children if they enjoyed the story. Ask: *Have you read any similar stories? Was the language, vocabulary and context simple or challenging? Why?* (The author uses simple language and vocabulary to make it accessible to younger readers so they can understand the challenging issues in the book.)

- Write some words (from the Word list) on the board: 'privilege', 'prejudice', 'opportunity', 'sacrifice'. Explain that these words might not actually appear in the story but they relate to the themes and dilemmas in the story. Check the meaning of the words and then invite the children to work in pairs and use them in sentences of their own.

- With discretion, write further words (from the Word list) on the board: 'category', 'controversy', 'desperate', 'determined', 'harass', 'correspond', 'hindrance', 'profession', 'system' and so on.

- Working in pairs, ask the children to look up the words in dictionaries, check the meaning then test their recall by taking turns to test each other on the meaning and spelling of each word. Ask: *Have you used these words before? Can you relate them to the themes in the story?* Invite suggestions.

- Working individually, ask the children to choose five words to use in sentences of their own, explaining some of the themes and dilemmas of the story and using different characters and scenarios as examples.

Differentiation

Support: Ask the children to work in groups, with each child focusing on one word only, then pool their ideas.

Extension: Ask the children to consider the words 'privilege' and 'prejudice' closely then discuss what each word means.

6. Naledi's journey

Objective

To make comparisons within and across books.

What you need

Copies of *Journey to Jo'burg*.

What to do

- Begin by recalling the idea of personal and physical journeys covered in previous activities. Ask: *What makes people grow?* (challenges or 'tests') *What words describe what happens if you don't grow?* ('shrink', 'stagnate', 'decline') Invite ideas.

- Invite the children to skim Chapters 1 and 15 to recap. Ask volunteers to describe the events and context of the beginning and end of the story. Ask: *How much time has passed from the first to the last chapter?* (about ten days altogether)

- Tell the children that they are going to look at how Naledi (and her situation) changes from the beginning to the end of the story. Write the following headings on the board: 'Her outside' (her situation and things around her); 'Her outlook' (how she views the world, her feelings, emotions, dreams and thoughts).

- Organise the children into groups to discuss, compare and make notes. Remind them to make links between the beginning and the end, and to mention specific events, people and ideas that affected Naledi and caused her to grow and to change her outlook – for example, meeting Grace, seeing Mma at her work, watching the police raid, learning about apartheid. Have a class feedback and discussion session.

- Working individually, ask the children to write a paragraph comparing Naledi at the beginning and the end of the story. Assess their ability to make comparisons and describe the changes that take place in Naledi.

Differentiation

Support: Provide sentence starters: 'At the beginning she thinks…', 'She plans…', 'At the end she realises…'.

Extension: Invite the children to predict what will happen to Naledi in the future then write a chapter about Naledi ten years on.

Grace's story

Read Chapter 10, then answer the questions carefully in your notebooks.

1. Who tells Grace's story?

2. Would you describe her story as a bedtime story? Why?

3. Who was Dumi?

4. Why were Dumi and the other children protesting?

5. What did the slogan on the banner mean?

6. How did the police respond to the protesting children?

7. Where did this occur?

8. Identify the sentence in Grace's story that links with her statement 'It was a "time of fire"'.

9. Find synonyms for the words 'lifted', 'sting', 'slaying'.

10. Find antonyms for the words 'peace', 'alive', 'appeared'.

11. How long did the family wait to hear from Dumi after he disappeared?

12. What did Dumi say he was doing?

13. How did the family feel about this?

14. In what way did Dumi change?

15. Based on the text, what do you think Dumi did later on? Write another chapter called 'Dumi's story' from Dumi's viewpoint on what happened to him.

SCHOLASTIC
READ & RESPOND

Available in this series:

978-1407-15879-2

978-1407-14224-1

978-1407-16063-4

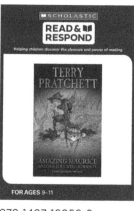

978-1407-16056-6

978-1407-14228-9

978-1407-16069-6

978-1407-16070-2

978-1407-16071-9

978-1407-14230-2

978-1407-16057-3

978-1407-16064-1

978-1407-14223-4

978-0702-30890-1

978-0702-30859-8

To find out more,
visit www.scholastic.co.uk/read-and-respond